BUSINESS MOTIVATION

:: Author ::

KINCHIT PARESHBHAI SHAH

(M.COM., C.A. – CPT., P.G.D.T.P(Gold Medalist)., SLET)

PUBLISHED BY

Hemchadracharya International Publishing House
HQ. At & Po. Chaveli., Ta- Chansma,
Dist- Patan, North Gujarat, India, Asia.
www.iphouseindia.com

BUSINESS MOTIVATION

First Publication: 22TH JANUARY, 2015

Copyright: Author
(c) KINCHIT PARESHBHAI SHAH

ISBN:- 978-15-08712-11-4

Price: Rs.750/- INDIA
   $ 15 OUTSIDE INDIA

PUBLISHED BY

Hemchadracharya International Publishing House
HQ. At & Po. Chaveli., Ta- Chansma,
Dist- Patan, North Gujarat, India, Asia.
www.iphouseindia.com

Dedicated
to
my
Parents

What is Motivation ?

Motivation is the word derived from the word 'motive' which means needs, desires, wants or drives within the individuals. It is the process of stimulating people to actions to accomplish the goals. In the work goal context the psychological factors stimulating the people's behaviour can be -

- desire for money
- success
- recognition
- job-satisfaction
- team work, etc

One of the most important functions of management is to create willingness amongst the employees to perform in the best of their abilities. Therefore the role of a leader is to arouse interest in performance of employees in their jobs. The process of motivation consists of three stages:-

1. A felt need or drive
2. A stimulus in which needs have to be aroused
3. When needs are satisfied, the satisfaction or accomplishment of goals.

Therefore, we can say that motivation is a psychological phenomenon which means needs and wants of the individuals have to be tackled by framing an incentive plan.

Maslow's Need Hierarchy Model

Human Behaviour is goal-directed. Motivation cause goal-directed behaviour. It is through motivation that needs can be handled and tackled purposely. This can be understood by understanding the hierarchy of needs by manager. The needs of individual serves as a driving force in human behaviour. Therefore, a manager must understand the "hierarchy of needs". Maslow has proposed "The Need Hierarchy Model".

Self-actualization Needs

Esteem Needs

Social Needs

Security

Needs

Physiological

Needs

FIGURE - Maslow's Need Hierarchy Model

The needs have been classified into the following in order:

1. **Physiological needs-** These are the basic needs of an individual which includes food, clothing, shelter, air, water, etc. These needs relate to the survival and maintenance of human life.

2. **Safety needs-** These needs are also important for human beings. Everybody wants job security, protection against danger, safety of property, etc.

3. **Social needs-** These needs emerge from society. Man is a social animal. These needs become important. For example- love, affection, belongingness, friendship, conversation, etc.

4. **Esteem needs-** These needs relate to desire for self-respect, recognition and respect from others.

5. **Self-actualization needs-** These are the needs of the highest order and these needs are found in those person whose previous four needs are satisfied. This will include need for social service, meditation.

Motivation Incentives - Incentives to motivate employees

Incentive is an act or promise for greater action. It is also called as a stimulus to greater action. Incentives are something which are given in addition to wagers. It means additional remuneration or benefit to an employee in recognition of achievement or better work. Incentives provide a spur or zeal in the employees for better performance. It is a natural thing that nobody acts without a purpose behind. Therefore, a hope for a reward is a powerful incentive to motivate employees. Besides monetary incentive, there are some other stimuli which can drive a person to better. This will include job satisfaction, job security, job promotion, and pride for accomplishment. Therefore, incentives really can sometimes work to accomplish the goals of a concern. The need of incentives can be many:-

1. To increase productivity,

2. To drive or arouse a stimulus work,

3. To enhance commitment in work performance,

4. To psychologically satisfy a person which leads to job satisfaction,

5. To shape the behavior or outlook of subordinate towards work,

6. To inculcate zeal and enthusiasm towards work,

7. To get the maximum of their capabilities so that they are exploited and utilized maximally.

Therefore, management has to offer the following two categories of incentives to motivate employees:

1. **Monetary incentives-** Those incentives which satisfy the subordinates by providing them rewards in terms of rupees. Money has been recognized as a chief source of satisfying the needs of people. Money is also helpful to satisfy the social needs by possessing various material items. Therefore, money not only satisfies psychological needs but also the security and social needs. Therefore, in many factories, various wage plans and bonus schemes are introduced to motivate and stimulate the people to work.

2. **Non-monetary incentives-** Besides the monetary incentives, there are certain non-financial incentives which can satisfy the ego and self- actualization needs of employees. The incentives which cannot be measured in terms of money are under the category of "Non- monetary incentives". Whenever a manager has to satisfy the psychological needs of the subordinates, he makes use of non-financial incentives. Non-financial incentives can be of the following types:-

   a. **Security of service-** Job security is an incentive which provides great motivation to employees. If his job is secured, he will put maximum efforts to achieve the objectives of the enterprise. This also helps since he is very far off from mental tension and he can give his best to the enterprise.

   b. **Praise or recognition-** The praise or recognition is another non- financial incentive which satisfies the ego needs of the employees. Sometimes praise becomes more effective than any other incentive. The employees will respond more to praise and try to give the best of their abilities to a concern.

c. **Suggestion scheme-** The organization should look forward to taking suggestions and inviting suggestion schemes from the subordinates. This inculcates a spirit of participation in the employees. This can be done by publishing various articles written by employees to improve the work environment which can be published in various magazines of the company. This also is helpful to motivate the employees to feel important and they can also be in search for innovative methods which can be applied for better work methods. This ultimately helps in growing a concern and adapting new methods of operations.

d. **Job enrichment-** Job enrichment is another non-monetary incentive in which the job of a worker can be enriched. This can be done by increasing his responsibilities, giving him an important designation, increasing the content and nature of the work. This way efficient worker can get challenging jobs in which they can prove their worth. This also helps in the greatest motivation of the efficient employees.

e. **Promotion opportunities-** Promotion is an effective tool to increase the spirit to work in a concern. If the employees are provided opportunities for the advancement and growth, they feel satisfied and contented and they become more committed to the organization.

The above non-financial tools can be framed effectively by giving due concentration to the role of employees. A combination of financial and non- financial incentives help together in bringing motivation and zeal to work in a concern.

Positive Incentives

Positive incentives are those incentives which provide a positive assurance for fulfilling the needs and wants. Positive incentives generally have an optimistic attitude behind and they are generally given to satisfy the psychological requirements of employees. For example- promotion, praise, recognition, perks and allowances, etc. It is positive by nature.

Negative Incentives

Negative incentives are those whose purpose is to correct the mistakes or defaults of employees. The purpose is to rectify mistakes in order to get effective results. Negative incentive is generally resorted to when positive incentive does not works and a psychological set back has to be given to employees. It is negative by nature. For example- demotion, transfer, fines, penalties.

Importance of Motivation

Motivation is a very important for an organization because of the following benefits it provides:-

1. Puts human resources into action

Every concern requires physical, financial and human resources to accomplish the goals. It is through motivation that the human resources can be utilized by making full use of it. This can be done by building willingness in employees to work. This will help the enterprise in securing best possible utilization of resources.

2. Improves level of efficiency of employees

The level of a subordinate or a employee does not only depend upon his qualifications and abilities. For getting best of his work performance, the gap between ability and willingness has to be filled which helps in improving the level of performance of subordinates. This will result into-

    a. Increase in productivity,

    b. Reducing cost of operations, and

    c. Improving overall efficiency.

3. Leads to achievement of organizational goals

The goals of an enterprise can be achieved only when the following factors take place :-

    a. There is best possible utilization of resources,

    b. There is a co-operative work environment,

    c. The employees are goal-directed and they act in a purposive manner,

    d. Goals can be achieved if co-ordination and co-operation takes place simultaneously which can be effectively done through motivation.

4. Builds friendly relationship

Motivation is an important factor which brings employees satisfaction. This can be done by keeping into mind and framing an incentive plan for the benefit of the employees. This could initiate the following things:

    a. Monetary and non-monetary incentives,

    b. Promotion opportunities for employees,

    c. Disincentives for inefficient employees.

In order to build a cordial, friendly atmosphere in a concern, the above steps should be taken by a manager. This would help in:

    iv. Effective co-operation which brings stability,

    v. Industrial dispute and unrest in employees will reduce,

    vi. The employees will be adaptable to the changes and there will be no resistance to the change,

    vii. This will help in providing a smooth and sound concern in which individual interests will coincide with the organizational interests,

    viii. This will result in profit maximization through increased productivity.

Leads to stability of work force

Stability of workforce is very important from the point of view of reputation and goodwill of a concern. The employees can remain loyal to the enterprise only when they have a feeling of participation in the management. The skills and efficiency of employees will always be of advantage to employees as well as employees. This will lead to a good public image in the market which will attract competent and qualified people into a concern. As it is said, "Old is gold" which suffices with the role of motivation here, the older the people, more the experience and their adjustment into a concern which can be of benefit to the enterprise.

From the above discussion, we can say that motivation is an internal feeling which can be understood only by manager since he is in close contact with the employees. Needs, wants and desires are inter-related and they are the driving force to act. These needs can be understood by the manager and he can framc motivation plans accordingly. We can say that motivation therefore is a continuous process since motivation process is based on needs which are unlimited. The process has to be continued throughout.

We can summarize by saying that motivation is important both to an individual and a business. **Motivation is important to an individual as:**

1. Motivation will help him achieve his personal goals.

2. If an individual is motivated, he will have job satisfaction.

3. Motivation will help in self-development of individual.

4. An individual would always gain by working with a dynamic team.

Similarly, **motivation is important to a business as:**

1. The more motivated the employees are, the more empowered the team is.

2. The more is the team work and individual employee contribution, more profitable and successful is the business.

3. During period of amendments, there will be more adaptability and creativity.

4. Motivation will lead to an optimistic and challenging attitude at work place.

Motivation and Morale - Relationship and Differences

Motivation can be defined as the total satisfaction derived by an individual from his job, his work-group, his superior, the organization he works for and the environment. It generally relates to the feeling of individual's comfort, happiness and satisfaction.

According to Davis, "Morale is a mental condition of groups and individuals which determines their attitude."

In short, morale is a fusion of employees' attitudes, behaviours, manifestation of views and opinions - all taken together in their work scenarios, exhibiting the employees' feelings towards work, working terms and relation with their employers. Morale includes employees' attitudes on and specific reaction to their job.

There are two states of morale:

igh morale - High morale implies determination at work- an essential in achievement of management objectives. High morale results in:

A keen teamwork on part of the employees.

Organizational Commitment and a sense of belongingness in the employees mind.

Immediate conflict identification and resolution.

Healthy and safe work environment.

Effective communication in the organization.

Increase in productivity.

Greater motivation.

Low morale - Low morale has following features:

Greater grievances and conflicts in organization.

High rate of employee absenteeism and turnover.

Dissatisfaction with the superiors and employers.

Poor working conditions.

Employees frustration.

Decrease in productivity.

Lack of motivation.

Though motivation and morale are closely related concepts, they are different in following ways:

While motivation is an internal-psychological drive of an individual which urges him to behave in a specific manner, morale is more of a group scenario.

Higher motivation often leads to higher morale of employees, but high morale does not essentially result in greatly motivated employees as to have a positive attitude towards all factors of work situation may not essentially force the employees to work more efficiently.

While motivation is an individual concept, morale is a group concept. Thus, motivation takes into consideration the individual differences among the employees, and morale of the employees can be increased by taking those factors into consideration which influence group scenario or total work settings.

Motivation acquires primary concern in every organization, while morale is a secondary phenomenon because high motivation essentially leads to higher productivity while high morale may not necessarily lead to higher productivity.

Things tied to morale are usually things that are just part of the work environment, and things tied to motivation are tied to the performance of the individual.

Staff Motivation - Motivation Tips for Employees

Employees are the building blocks of an organization. Organizational success depends on the collective efforts of the employees. The employees will collectively contribute to organizational growth when they are motivated.

Below mentioned are some tips for motivating the staff/employees in an organization:

Evaluate yourself- In order to motivate, encourage and control your staff's behaviour, it is essential to understand, encourage and control your own behaviour as a manager. Work upon utilizing your strengths and opportunities to neutralize and lower the negative impact of your weaknesses and organizational threats. The manager should adopt the approach "You're OK - I'm OK".

Be familiar with your staff- The manager should be well acquainted with his staff. The more and the better he knows his staff, the simpler it is to get them involved in the job as well as in achieving the team and organizational goals. This will also invite staff's commitment and loyalty. A cordial superior-subordinate relationship is a key factor in job-satisfaction.

Provide the employees certain benefits- Give your staff some financial and other benefits. Give them bonuses, pay them for overtime, and give them health and family insurance benefits. Make sure they get breaks from work. Let them enjoy vacations and holidays.

Participate in new employees induction programme- Induction proceeds with recruitment advertising. At this point of time, the potential entrants start creating their own impressions and desires about the job and the organization. The manner in which the selection is conducted and the consequent recruitment process will either build or damage the impression about the job and organization. Thus, the manager must have a say in framing the advertisement and also in the selection and recruitment process. After the decision about the candidate is made, the manager must take personal interest in the selected joinee's joining date, the family relocation issues, cost of removal, etc. Being observed by the new recruit and your entire team / staff to be involved completely, will ensure a persuasive entry in the organization.

Provide feedback to the staff constantly- The staff members are keen to know how they are performing. Try giving a regular and constructive feedback to your staff. This will be more acceptable by the staff. Do not base the feedback on assumptions, but on facts and personal observations. Do not indulge in favouritism or comparing the employee with some one else. Sit with your staff on daily or weekly basis and make sure that feedback happens. This will help in boosting employee's morale and will thus motivate the staff.

Acknowledge your staff on their achievements- A pat on the back, some words of praise, and giving a note of credit to the employee / staff member at personal level with some form of broad publicity can motivate the staff a lot. Make it a point to mention the staff's outstanding achievements in official newsletters or organization's journal. Not only acknowledge the employee with highest contribution, but also acknowledge the employee who meets and over exceeds the targets.

Ensure effective time management- Having control over time ensures that things are done in right manner. Motivate your staff to have "closed" times, i.e., few hours when there are no interruptions for the staff in performing their job role so that they can concentrate on the job, and "open" times when the staff freely communicate and interact. Plan one to one sessions of interaction with your staff where they can ask their queries and also can get your attention and, thereby, they will not feel neglected. This all will work in long run to motivate the staff.

Have stress management techniques in your organization- Create an environment in which you and your staff can work within optimum pressure levels. Ensure an optimistic attitude towards stress in the workplace. Have training sessions on stress management, and ensure a follow-up with group meetings on the manner stress can be lowered at work. Give your staff autonomy in work. Identify the stress symptoms in employees and try to deal with them.

Use counselling technique- The employees' / staff feelings towards the work, their peer, their superiors and towards the future can be effectively dealt through the staff counseling. Counselling provides an environment, incentive and support which enable the employee to achieve his identity.

Give the employees learning opportunities- Employees should consistently learn new skills on the job. It has been well said by someone that with people hopping jobs more often than required and organizations no longer giving job security to employees, the young blood employees specifically realize that continuing learning is the best way to remain employable. Opportunities should be given to the employees to develop their skills and competencies and to make best use of their skills. Link the staff goals with the organizational goals.

Set an example for your staff / subordinates- Be a role model for your staff. The staff would learn from what you do and not from what you say / claim. The way you interact with your clients / customers and how do you react later after the interaction is over have an impact upon the staff. The staff more closely observes your non-verbal communication (gestures, body language). Being unpunctual, wasting the organization's capital, mismanaging organization's physical equipments, asking the staff to do your personal work, etc. all have a negative impact on the staff. Try setting an example for your staff to follow.

Smile often- Smiling can have a tremendous effect on boosting the morale of the staff. A smiling superior creates an optimistic and motivating work environment. Smiling is an essential component of the body language of confidence, acceptance and boldness. Smile consistently, naturally and often, to demonstrate that you feel good and positive about the staff who works for you. It encourages new ideas and feedback from the staff. The staff does not feel hesitant and threatened to discuss their views this way.

Listen effectively- Listening attentively is a form of recognizing and appreciating the person who is talking. Reciprocal / Mutual listening develops cordial and healthy personal relationships on which the employee / staff development rests. If the managers do not listen attentively to the subordinates, the morale of the subordinates lowers down and they do not feel like sharing their ideas or giving their views. Effective listening by the manager boosts up the employees' morale and thus motivates them.

Ensure effective communication- In order to motivate your staff, indulge in effective communication such as avoid using anger expressions, utilize questioning techniques to know staff's mindset and analysis rather than ordering the staff what to do, base your judgements on facts and not on assumptions, use relaxed and steady tone of voice, listen effectively and be positive and helpful in your responses. Share your views with the staff.

Develop and encourage creativity- The staff should be encouraged to develop the creativity skills so as to solve organizational problems. Give them time and resources for developing creativity. Let them hold constant brainstorming sessions. Invite ideas and suggestions from the staff. They may turn out to be very productive.

Don't be rigid. Be flexible- Introduce flexibility in work. Allow for flexible working hours if possible. Let the employees work at home occasionally if need arises. Do not be rigid in accepting ideas from your staff. Stimulate flexible attitudes in the employees who are accountable to you by asking what changes they would like to bring about if given a chance.

Adopt job enrichment- Job enrichment implies giving room for a better quality of working life. It means facilitating people to achieve self-development, fame and success through a more challenging and interesting job which provides more promotional and advancement opportunities. Give employees more freedom in job, involve them in decision-making process, show them loyalty and celebrate their achievements.

Respect your team- Respect not only the employees' rights to share and express their views, and to be themselves, but their time too. This will ensure that the employees respect you and your time. Make the staff feel that they are respected not just as employees / workers but as individuals too.

Workplace Motivation - Carrot or Stick approach doesn't work anymore

"I am in this job because I have no other option." If this is what an employee of your company feels, read on to know how this statement can be changed to something more positive - "I love what I do."

First things first - whose responsibility is it to ensure that an employee loves his job? While an employee would say - the employer, the human resource experts have a different point of view which sounds fair. It's both the employer and the employee who should work together to make work fun for each other.

It is interesting to know here, that employees do not rank 'salary' as the top factor in determining whether they like their jobs or not. What is important to them then - the opportunity to do what is 'important'. Almost all the employees would like to feel part of the big picture and would want to contribute to the organizational goals in some way or the other. Doing the mundane, routine work will never excite them - what excites them is - work that challenges them to use their talent. Right Management Consultants conducted a survey sometime back and found that 83% of about 500 workers surveyed were motivated by "challenges at work".

Also, as per an executive editor of the Harvard Business Review, while salary and promotions could do a great job of demotivating people if handled ineffectively, they aren't so much effective in motivating people.

So then what needs to be done for effective motivation at workplace?

✓ **Link Rewards directly to Performance-** An organization should adopt a fair reward structure which provides incentive to the most deserving employee. Have an incentive structure in place doesn't solve the problem... what makes it workable is the employees trust in the system and believe that they will be rewarded if they perform well.

✓ **Compliment employees-** Even though an employee's name has not appeared in the list of people getting incentives, go ahead and compliment that employee for a job well done - no matter how small. There is nothing more satisfying to an employee than a pat on his back.

✓ **Be transparent-** While there may be some strategic decisions which you might want to share with the employees at a later stage, make sure employees do not give in to the rumours. Stay in touch with the employees.

✓ **Work on your PDP-** Every employee is responsible for his / her own career. He / she should work towards his 'Personal Development Plan' [PDP] as discussed and agreed by his manager. Find out what are the training company offers and which is best suited to his development needs. How this will motivate you - remember training always increase your marketability and enhance your career.

✓ **Participate and Network-** Employees - Remember you

work for a company where a one-on-one attention might not be possible. Do not wait for an invitation to participate in a discussion. If you are a part of a forum, then you have full right to express your opinion and be a part of the process. Expressing yourself is a good way of motivating yourself.

Self Motivation at Work

Self-motivation is a power that drives us to keep moving ahead. It encourages continuous learning and success, whatever be the scenario. Self-motivation is a primary means of realizing our goals and progressing. It is basically related to our inventiveness in setting dynamic goals for ourselves, and our faith that we possess the required skills and competencies for achieving those challenging goals. We often feel the need for self-motivation.

Following are the ways/techniques for self-motivation:

Communicate and talk to get motivated: Communicating with someone can boost up your energy and make you go on track. Talk with optimistic and motivated individuals. They can be your colleagues, friends, wife, or any one with whom you can share your ideas.

Remain optimistic: When facing hurdles; we always make efforts to find how to overcome them. Also, one should understand the good in bad.

Discover your interest area: If you lack interest in current task, you should not proceed and continue with it. If an individual has no interest in the task, but if it is essential to perform, he should correlate it with a bigger ultimate goal.

Self-acknowledgement: One should know when his motivation level is saturated and he feels like on top of the world. There will be a blueprint that once an individual acknowledge, he can proceed with his job and can grow.

Monitor and record your success: Maintain a success bar for the assignments you are currently working on. When you observe any progress, you will obviously want to foster it.

Uplift energy level: Energy is very essential for self-motivation. Do regular exercises. Have proper sleep. Have tea/coffee during breaks to refresh you.

Assist, support and motivate others: Discuss and share your views and ideas with your friends and peers and assist them in getting motivated. When we observe others performing good, it will keep us motivated too. Invite feedback from others on your achievements.

Encourage learning: Always encourage learning. Read and grasp the logic and jist of the reading. Learning makes an individual more confident in commencing new assignments.

Break your bigger goals into smaller goals: Set a short time deadline for each smaller goal so as to achieve bigger goal on time.

Team Motivation - Tips for Motivating Team

A group heading towards a common objective will perform best when it is motivated as a team. Team motivation is determined by how well the team members' needs and requirements are met by the team.

Some tips for effective team motivation are as follows:

The team's objective should well align and synchronize with the team members needs and requirements.

Give in written the team's mission and ensure that all understand it (as mission is a foundation based on which the team performs).

For maintaining motivation, the team should be given challenges (which must be difficult but achievable) consistently.

Giving a team responsibility accompanied by authority can also be a good motivator for the team to perform.

The team should be provided with growth opportunities. The team's motivation level is high when the team members feel that they are being promoted, their skills and competencies are being enhanced, and they are learning new things consistently.

Effective and true leaders can develop environment for the team to motivate itself. They provide spur for self-actualization behaviours of team members.

Devote quality/productive time to your team. Have an optimistic and good relation with your team members. This will make you more acquainted with them and you can get knowledge of how well they are performing their job.

Welcome their views and ideas as they may be fruitful and it will also boost their morale.

Motivation is all about empowerment. The skills and competencies of the team members should be fully utilized. Empowering the team members makes them accountable for their own actions.

Provide feedback to the team consistently. Become their mentor. Give the team recognition for good and outstanding performance. Give the team a constructive and not negative feedback.

Discover and offset the factors which discourage team spirit such as too many conflicts, lethargy, team members' escape from responsibilities, lack of job satisfaction, etc.

The Role of Motivation in Organizational Behavior

Motivation and Organizational Theory

Though we have discussed motivation extensively earlier, the role of the HR department and the role of the organizational culture in motivating employees have not been discussed at length. As organizational theory states, employees need to be motivated to actualize their potential and there are several ways of enabling them and empowering them to do so. These include the role of reward systems in motivating employees according to their needs for extrinsic or external motivation and by providing them opportunities that appeal to their intrinsic or internal motivation needs. The other factors that motivate employees are the kind of job that they are asked to perform, the added benefits like extended vacations and perquisites like company provided accommodation and funding for kids schooling as well as provision of medical insurance coverage for the employees and their families. In recent years, there has been lot of emphasis on motivating employees by organizing offsite events and fun and recreation events where the employees let their hair down and indulge in the much-needed stress relieving activities. Further, many employees are motivated because of the presence of famous business leaders in the top management of the company as is the case with Apple, Microsoft, Infosys, and the TATA Group.

Some Factors that can Motivate Employees

The organizational structure is another aspect that can motivate employees. For instance, it has been found that flat organizations as opposed to hierarchical organizations motivate employees more. Next, the organizational culture plays an important role in motivating employees. The examples of Google, Facebook, and startup companies where the organizational culture is open and collegiate are relevant in this regard. Third, the HR managers have an important role to play in motivating employees by interacting with them, finding their grievances, and proposing solutions to behavioral problems. There are many multinationals like Fidelity where the HR managers hold one on one sessions with the employees to foster an open and inclusive culture where employees do not hold anything back and where they are encouraged to be as forthright as possible. Fourth, organizations that promote diversity as an organizational imperative are known to motivate women employees who feel less threatened and less insecure than in organizations where bias and prejudice are rampant. Fifth, many organizations have the habit of saying one thing and doing something else altogether which means that they are hypocritical in their approach. Such organizations cannot motivate the employees particularly at the lower levels since the fresh recruits and those with less experience often look to the senior managers and the leadership for integrity and consistency.

Salary and Benefits are not the only Motivators

Having covered the various aspects of how the organizations can motivate the employees, it needs to be mentioned that mere reliance on salary and benefits cannot motivate employees completely. With the advent of the software and services sector, the attraction of being sent onsite has become an important motivator for the employees who when given the chance to go onsite ramp up on their performance noticeably. Apart from this, the fact that the brand image of the organization makes a lot of difference to the motivation levels of the employees is another factor. For instance, many graduates have their own preferences for dream companies or companies that they would like to work in after graduation. This important motivator attracts the best talent to those companies that are often viewed as the benchmark for industry peers. Of course, if the image does not meet up to reality or if the hype is without substance, many employees lose motivation to work in such companies.

Concluding Thoughts

Finally, as discussed above, there is no set formula on what organizations can do or cannot do to motivate the employees. The best approach would be to let employees find their own niche within the organization and let them actualize their potential instead of forcing them to do work that is not to their liking. Apart from this, many industry veterans are also of the view that employees have to find their company that suits them and hence, clinging on to jobs that do not motivate them is counterproductive.

Motivational Challenges

Motivation seems to be a simple function of management in books, but in practice it is more challenging. **The reasons for motivation being challenging job are as follows:**

- One of the main reasons of motivation being a challenging job is due to the changing workforce. The employees become a part of their organization with various needs and expectations. Different employees have different beliefs, attitudes, values, backgrounds and thinking. But all the organizations are not aware of the diversity in their workforce and thus are not aware and clear about different ways of motivating their diverse workforce.

- Employees motives cannot be seen, they can only be presumed. Suppose, there are two employees in a team showing varying performance despite being of same age group, having same educational qualifications and same work experience. The reason being what motivates one employee may not seem motivating to other.

- Motivation of employees becomes challenging especially when the organizations have considerably changed the job role of the employees, or have lessened the hierarchy levels of hierarchy, or have chucked out a significant number of employees in the name of down-sizing or right-sizing. Certain firms have chosen to hire and fire and paying for performance strategies nearly giving up motivational efforts. These strategies are unsuccessful in making an individual overreach himself.

· The vigorous nature of needs also pose challenge to a manager in motivating his subordinates. This is because an employee at a certain point of time has diverse needs and expectations. Also, these needs and expectations keep on changing and might also clash with each other. For instance-the employees who spend extra time at work for meeting their needs for accomplishment might discover that the extra time spent by them clash with their social neds and with the need for affiliation.

Essentials / Features of a Good Motivation System

Motivation is a state of mind. High motivation leads to high morale and greater production. A motivated employee gives his best to the organization. He stays loyal and committed to the organization. A sound motivation system in an organization should have the following features:

Superior performance should be reasonably rewarded and should be duely acknowledged. If the performance is not consistently up to the mark, then the system must make provisions for penalties.

The employees must be dealt in a fair and just manner. The grievances and obstacles faced by them must be dealt instantly and fairly.

Carrot and stick approach should be implemented to motivate both efficient and inefficient employees. The employees should treat negative consequences (such as fear of punishment) as stick, an outside push and move away from it. They should take positive consequences (such as reward) as carrot, an inner pull and move towards it.

Performance appraisal system should be very effective.

Ensure flexibility in working arrangements.

A sound motivation system must be correlated to organizational goals. Thus, the individual/employee goals must be harmonized with the organizational goals.

The motivational system must be modified to the situation and to the organization.

A sound motivation system requires modifying the nature of individual's jobs. The jobs should be redesigned or restructured according to the requirement of situation. Any of the alternatives to job specialization - job rotation, job enlargement, job enrichment, etc. could be used.

The management approach should be participative. All the subordinates and employees should be involved in decision- making process.

The motivation system should involve monetary as well as non- monetary rewards. The monetary rewards should be correlated to performance. Performance should be based on the employees' action towards the goals, and not on the fame of employees.

"Motivate yourself to motivate your employees" should be the managerial approach.

The managers must understand and identify the motivators for each employee.

Sound motivation system should encourage supportive supervision whereby the supervisors share their views and experiences with their subordinates, listen to the subordinates views, and assist the subordinates in performing the designated job.

Classical Theories of Motivation

The motivation concepts were mainly developed around 1950's. Three main theories were made during this period. These three classical theories are-

Maslow's hierarchy of needs theory

Herzberg's Two factor theory

Theory X and Theory Y

These theories are building blocks of the contemporary theories developed later. The working mangers and learned professionals till date use these classical theories to explain the concept of employee motivation.

Maslow's Hierarchy of Needs Theory

Abraham Maslow is well renowned for proposing the Hierarchy of Needs Theory in 1943. This theory is a classical depiction of human motivation. This theory is based on the assumption that there is a hierarchy of five needs within each individual. The urgency of these needs varies. These five needs are as follows- Physiological needs- These are the basic needs of air, water, food, clothing and shelter. In other words, physiological needs are the needs for basic amenities of life.

Safety needs- Safety needs include physical, environmental and emotional safety and protection. For instance- Job security, financial security, protection from animals, family security, health security, etc.

Social needs- Social needs include the need for love, affection, care, belongingness, and friendship.

Esteem needs- Esteem needs are of two types: internal esteem needs (self- respect, confidence, competence, achievement and freedom) and external esteem needs (recognition, power, status, attention and admiration).

Self-actualization need- This include the urge to become what you are capable of becoming / what you have the potential to become. It includes the need for growth and self-contentment. It also includes desire for gaining more knowledge, social- service, creativity and being aesthetic. The self- actualization needs are never fully satiable. As an individual grows psychologically, opportunities keep cropping up to continue growing.

According to Maslow, individuals are motivated by unsatisfied needs. As each of these needs is significantly satisfied, it drives and forces the next need to emerge. Maslow grouped the five needs into two categories - Higher-order needs and Lower-order needs. The physiological and the safety needs constituted the lower-order needs. These lower-order needs are mainly satisfied externally. The social, esteem, and self-actualization needs constituted the higher-order needs. These higher-order needs are generally satisfied internally, i.e., within an individual. Thus, we can conclude that during boom period, the employees lower-order needs are significantly met.

Implications of Maslow's Hierarchy of Needs Theory for Managers

As far as the physiological needs are concerned, the managers should give employees appropriate salaries to purchase the basic necessities of life. Breaks and eating opportunities should be given to employees.

As far as the safety needs are concerned, the managers should provide the employees job security, safe and hygienic work environment, and retirement benefits so as to retain them.

As far as social needs are concerned, the management should encourage teamwork and organize social events.

As far as esteem needs are concerned, the managers can appreciate and reward employees on accomplishing and exceeding their targets. The management can give the deserved employee higher job rank / position in the organization.

As far as self-actualization needs are concerned, the managers can give the employees challenging jobs in which the employees' skills and competencies are fully utilized. Moreover, growth opportunities can be given to them so that they can reach the peak.

The managers must identify the need level at which the employee is existing and then those needs can be utilized as push for motivation.

Limitations of Maslow's Theory

It is essential to note that not all employees are governed by same set of needs. Different individuals may be driven by different needs at same point of time. It is always the most powerful unsatisfied need that motivates an individual.

The theory is not empirically supported.

The theory is not applicable in case of starving artist as even if the artist's basic needs are not satisfied, he will still strive for recognition and achievement.

Herzberg's Two-Factor Theory of Motivation

In 1959, Frederick Herzberg, a behavioural scientist proposed a two-factor theory or the motivator-hygiene theory. According to Herzberg, there are some job factors that result in satisfaction while there are other job factors that prevent dissatisfaction. According to Herzberg, the opposite of "Satisfaction" is "No satisfaction" and the opposite of "Dissatisfaction" is "No Dissatisfaction".

Herzbergs view of satisfaction and dissatisfaction

Herzberg classified these job factors into two categories-

Hygiene factors- Hygiene factors are those job factors which are essential for existence of motivation at workplace. These do not lead to positive satisfaction for long-term. But if these factors are absent / if these factors are non-existant at workplace, then they lead to dissatisfaction. In other words, hygiene factors are those factors which when adequate/reasonable in a job, pacify the employees and do not make them dissatisfied. These factors are extrinsic to work. Hygiene factors are also called as dissatisfiers or maintenance factors as they are required to avoid dissatisfaction. These factors describe the job environment/scenario. The hygiene factors symbolized the physiological needs which the individuals wanted and expected to be fulfilled. Hygiene factors include:

Pay - The pay or salary structure should be appropriate and reasonable. It must be equal and competitive to those in the same industry in the same domain.

Company Policies and administrative policies - The company policies should not be too rigid. They should be fair and clear. It should include flexible working hours, dress code, breaks, vacation, etc.

Fringe benefits - The employees should be offered health care plans (mediclaim), benefits for the family members, employee help programmes, etc.

Physical Working conditions - The working conditions should be safe, clean and hygienic. The work equipments should be updated and well-maintained.

Status - The employees' status within the organization should be familiar and retained.

Interpersonal relations - The relationship of the employees with his peers, superiors and subordinates should be appropriate and acceptable. There should be no conflict or humiliation element present.

Job Security - The organization must provide job security to the employees.

Motivational factors- According to Herzberg, the hygiene factors cannot be regarded as motivators. The motivational factors yield positive satisfaction. These factors are inherent to work. These factors motivate the employees for a superior performance. These factors are called satisfiers. These are factors involved in performing the job. Employees find these factors intrinsically rewarding. The motivators symbolized the psychological needs that were perceived as an additional benefit. Motivational factors include:

Recognition - The employees should be praised and recognized for their accomplishments by the managers.

Sense of achievement - The employees must have a sense of achievement. This depends on the job. There must be a fruit of some sort in the job.

Growth and promotional opportunities - There must be growth and advancement opportunities in an organization to motivate the employees to perform well.

Responsibility - The employees must hold themselves responsible for the work. The managers should give them ownership of the work. They should minimize control but retain accountability.

Meaningfulness of the work - The work itself should be meaningful, interesting and challenging for the employee to perform and to get motivated.

Limitations of Two-Factor Theory

The two factor theory is not free from limitations:

The two-factor theory overlooks situational variables.

Herzberg assumed a correlation between satisfaction and productivity. But the research conducted by Herzberg stressed upon satisfaction and ignored productivity.

The theory's reliability is uncertain. Analysis has to be made by the raters. The raters may spoil the findings by analyzing same response in different manner.

No comprehensive measure of satisfaction was used. An employee may find his job acceptable despite the fact that he may hate/object part of his job.

The two factor theory is not free from bias as it is based on the natural reaction of employees when they are enquired the sources of satisfaction and dissatisfaction at work. They will blame dissatisfaction on the external factors such as salary structure, company policies and peer relationship. Also, the employees will give credit to themselves for the satisfaction factor at work.

The theory ignores blue-collar workers. Despite these limitations, Herzberg's Two-Factor theory is acceptable broadly.

Implications of Two-Factor Theory

The Two-Factor theory implies that the managers must stress upon guaranteeing the adequacy of the hygiene factors to avoid employee dissatisfaction. Also, the managers must make sure that the work is stimulating and rewarding so that the employees are motivated to work and perform harder and better. This theory emphasize upon job-enrichment so as to motivate the employees. The job must utilize the employee's skills and competencies to the maximum. Focusing on the motivational factors can improve work-quality.

Theory X and Theory Y

In 1960, Douglas McGregor formulated Theory X and Theory Y suggesting two aspects of human behaviour at work, or in other words, two different views of individuals (employees): one of which is negative, called as Theory X and the other is positive, so called as Theory Y. According to McGregor, the perception of managers on the nature of individuals is based on various assumptions.

Assumptions of Theory X

An average employee intrinsically does not like work and tries to escape it whenever possible.

Since the employee does not want to work, he must be persuaded, compelled, or warned with punishment so as to achieve organizational goals. A close supervision is required on part of managers. The managers adopt a more dictatorial style.

Many employees rank job security on top, and they have little or no aspiration/ ambition.

Employees generally dislike responsibilities.

Employees resist change.

An average employee needs formal direction.

Assumptions of Theory Y

Employees can perceive their job as relaxing and normal. They exercise their physical and mental efforts in an inherent manner in their jobs.

Employees may not require only threat, external control and coercion to work, but they can use self-direction and self-control if they are dedicated and sincere to achieve the organizational objectives.

If the job is rewarding and satisfying, then it will result in employees' loyalty and commitment to organization.

An average employee can learn to admit and recognize the responsibility. In fact, he can even learn to obtain responsibility.

The employees have skills and capabilities. Their logical capabilities should be fully utilized. In other words, the creativity, resourcefulness and innovative potentiality of the employees can be utilized to solve organizational problems.

Thus, we can say that Theory X presents a pessimistic view of employees' nature and behaviour at work, while Theory Y presents an optimistic view of the employees' nature and behaviour at work. If correlate it with Maslow's theory, we can say that Theory X is based on the assumption that the employees emphasize on the physiological needs and the safety needs; while Theory X is based on the assumption that the social needs, esteem needs and the self-actualization needs dominate the employees.

McGregor views Theory Y to be more valid and reasonable than Theory X. Thus, he encouraged cordial team relations, responsible and stimulating jobs, and participation of all in decision-making process.

Implications of Theory X and Theory Y

Quite a few organizations use Theory X today. Theory X encourages use of tight control and supervision. It implies that employees are reluctant to organizational changes. Thus, it does not encourage innovation.

Many organizations are using Theory Y techniques. Theory Y implies that the managers should create and encourage a work environment which provides opportunities to employees to take initiative and self-direction. Employees should be given opportunities to contribute to organizational well-being. Theory Y encourages decentralization of authority, teamwork and participative decision making in an organization. Theory Y searches and discovers the ways in which an employee can make significant contributions in an organization. It harmonizes and matches employees' needs and aspirations with organizational needs and aspirations.

Modern Theories of Motivation

We all are familiar with the classical theories of motivation, but they all are not empirically supported. As far as contemporary theories of motivation are concerned, all are well supported with evidences. Some of the contemporary / modern theories of motivation are explained below:

ERG Theory

McClelland's Theory of Needs

Goal Setting Theory

Reinforcement Theory

Equity Theory of Motivation

Expectancy Theory of Motivation

ERG Theory of Motivation

To bring Maslow's need hierarchy theory of motivation in synchronization with empirical research, Clayton Alderfer redefined it in his own terms. His rework is called as ERG theory of motivation. He recategorized Maslow's hierarchy of needs into three simpler and broader classes of needs:

- **Existence needs-** These include need for basic material necessities. In short, it includes an individual's physiological and physical safety needs.

- **Relatedness needs-** These include the aspiration individual's have for maintaining significant interpersonal relationships (be it with family, peers or superiors), getting public fame and recognition. Maslow's social needs and external component of esteem needs fall under this class of need.

- **Growth needs-** These include need for self-development and personal growth and advancement. Maslow's self-actualization needs and intrinsic component of esteem needs fall under this category of need.

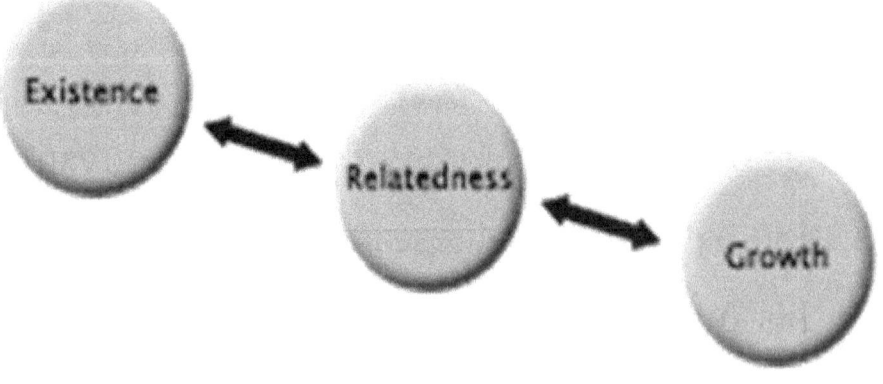

The significance of the three classes of needs may vary for each individual.

Difference between Maslow Need Hierarchy Theory and Alderfer's ERG Theory

✓ ERG Theory states that at a given point of time, more than one need may be operational.

✓ ERG Theory also shows that if the fulfillment of a higher-level need is subdued, there is an increase in desire for satisfying a lower-level need.

✓ According to Maslow, an individual remains at a particular need level until that need is satisfied. While according to ERG theory, if a higher- level need aggravates, an individual may revert to increase the satisfaction of a lower- level need. This is called frustration- regression aspect of ERG theory. For instance- when growth need aggravates, then an individual might be motivated to accomplish the relatedness need and if there are issues in accomplishing relatedness needs, then he might be motivated by the existence needs. Thus, frustration/aggravation can result in regression to a lower-level need.

✓ While Maslow's need hierarchy theory is rigid as it assumes that the needs follow a specific and orderly hierarchy and unless a lower-level need is satisfied, an individual cannot proceed to the higher-level need; ERG Theory of motivation is very flexible as he perceived the needs as a range/variety rather than perceiving them as a hierarchy. According to Alderfer, an individual can work on growth needs even if his existence or relatedness needs remain unsatisfied. Thus, he gives explanation to the issue of "starving artist" who can struggle for growth even if he is hungry.

Implications of the ERG Theory

Managers must understand that an employee has various needs that must be satisfied at the same time. According to the ERG theory, if the manager concentrates solely on one need at a time, this will not effectively motivate the employee. Also, the frustration- regression aspect of ERG Theory has an added effect on workplace motivation. For instance- if an employee is not provided with growth and advancement opportunities in an organization, he might revert to the relatedness need such as socializing needs and to meet those socializing needs, if the environment or circumstances do not permit, he might revert to the need for money to fulfill those socializing needs. The sooner the manager realizes and discovers this, the more immediate steps they will take to fulfill those needs which are frustrated until such time that the employee can again pursue growth.

Expectancy Theory of Motivation

The expectancy theory was proposed by Victor Vroom of Yale School of Management in 1964. Vroom stresses and focuses on outcomes, and not on needs unlike Maslow and Herzberg. The theory states that the intensity of a tendency to perform in a particular manner is dependent on the intensity of an expectation that the performance will be followed by a definite outcome and on the appeal of the outcome to the individual.

The Expectancy theory states that employee's motivation is an outcome of how much an individual wants a reward (Valence), the assessment that the likelihood that the effort will lead to expected performance (Expectancy) and the belief that the performance will lead to reward

(Instrumentality). In short, Valence is the significance associated by an individual about the expected outcome. It is an expected and not the actual satisfaction that an employee expects to receive after achieving the goals. Expectancy is the faith that better efforts will result in better performance. Expectancy is influenced by factors such as possession of appropriate skills for performing the job, availability of right resources, availability of crucial information and getting the required support for completing the job.

Instrumentality is the faith that if you perform well, then a valid outcome will be there. Instrumentality is affected by factors such as believe in the people who decide who receives what outcome, the simplicity of the process deciding who gets what outcome, and clarity of relationship between performance and outcomes. Thus, the expectancy theory concentrates on the following three relationships: Effort-performance relationship: What is the likelihood that the individual's effort be recognized in his performance appraisal?

Performance-reward relationship: It talks about the

extent to which the employee believes that getting a good performance appraisal leads to organizational rewards.

Rewards-personal goals relationship: It is all about the attractiveness or appeal of the potential reward to the individual.

Vroom was of view that employees consciously decide whether to perform or not at the job. This decision solely depended on the employee's motivation level which in turn depends on three factors of expectancy, valence and instrumentality.

Advantages of the Expectancy Theory

It is based on self-interest individual who want to achieve maximum satisfaction and who wants to minimize dissatisfaction.

This theory stresses upon the expectations and perception; what is real and actual is immaterial.

It emphasizes on rewards or pay-offs.

It focuses on psychological extravagance where final objective of individual is to attain maximum pleasure and least pain.

Limitations of the Expectancy Theory

The expectancy theory seems to be idealistic because quite a few individuals perceive high degree correlation between performance and rewards.

The application of this theory is limited as reward is not directly correlated with performance in many organizations. It is related to other parameters also such as position, effort, responsibility, education, etc.

Implications of the Expectancy Theory

The managers can correlate the preferred outcomes to the aimed performance levels.

The managers must ensure that the employees can achieve the aimed performance levels.

The deserving employees must be rewarded for their exceptional performance.

The reward system must be fair and just in an organization.

Organizations must design interesting, dynamic and challenging jobs.

The employee's motivation level should be continually assessed through various techniques such as questionnaire, personal interviews, etc.

McClelland's Theory of Needs

David McClelland and his associates proposed McClelland's theory of Needs / Achievement Motivation Theory. This theory states that human behaviour is affected by three needs - Need for Power, Achievement and Affiliation. Need for **achievement** is the urge to excel, to accomplish in relation to a set of standards, to struggle to achieve success. Need for **power** is the desire to influence other individual's behaviour as per your wish. In other words, it is the desire to have control over others and to be influential. Need for **affiliation** is a need for open and sociable interpersonal relationships. In other words, it is a desire for relationship based on co-operation and mutual understanding.

The individuals with high achievement needs are highly motivated by competing and challenging work. They look for promotional opportunities in job. They have a strong urge for feedback on their achievement. Such individuals try to get satisfaction in performing things better. High achievement is directly related to high performance. Individuals who are better and above average performers are highly motivated. They assume responsibility for solving the problems at work. McClelland called such individuals as gamblers as they set challenging targets

for themselves and they take deliberate risk to achieve those set targets. Such individuals look for innovative ways of performing job. They perceive achievement of goals as a reward, and value it more than a financial reward.

The individuals who are motivated by power have a strong urge to be influential and controlling. They want that their views and ideas should dominate and thus, they want to lead. Such individuals are motivated by the need for reputation and self-esteem. Individuals with greater power and authority will perform better than those possessing less power. Generally, managers with high need for power turn out to be more efficient and successful managers. They are more determined and loyal to the organization they work for. Need for power should not always be taken negatively. It can be viewed as the need to have a positive effect on the organization and to support the organization in achieving it's goals.

The individuals who are motivated by affiliation have an urge for a friendly and supportive environment. Such individuals are effective performers in a team. These people want to be liked by others. The manager's ability to make decisions is hampered if they have a high affiliation need as they prefer to be accepted and liked by others, and this weakens their objectivity. Individuals having high affiliation needs prefer working in an environment providing greater personal interaction. Such people have a need to be on the good books of all. They generally cannot be good leaders.

Goal Setting Theory of Motivation

In 1960's, **Edwin Locke** put forward the Goal-setting theory of motivation. This theory states that goal setting is essentially linked to task performance. It states that specific and challenging goals along with appropriate feedback contribute to higher and better task performance. In simple words, goals indicate and give direction to an employee about what needs to be done and how much efforts are required to be put in. The important **features of goal-setting theory** are as follows:

✓ The willingness to work towards attainment of goal is main source of job motivation. Clear, particular and difficult goals are greater motivating factors than easy, general and vague goals.

✓ **Specific and clear** goals lead to greater output and better performance. Unambiguous, measurable and clear goals accompanied by a deadline for completion avoids misunderstanding.

✓ Goals should be **realistic and challenging**. This gives an individual a feeling of pride and triumph when he attains them, and sets him up for attainment of next goal. The more challenging the goal, the greater is the reward generally and the more is the passion for achieving it.

✓ Better and appropriate feedback of results directs the employee behaviour and contributes to higher performance than absence of feedback. Feedback is a means of gaining reputation, making clarifications and regulating goal difficulties. It helps employees to work with more involvement and leads to greater job satisfaction.

✓ **Employees' participation** in goal is not always desirable.

✓ Participation of setting goal, however, makes goal more

acceptable and leads to more involvement.

✓ Goal setting theory has certain eventualities such as:

    a. **Self-efficiency-** Self-efficiency is the individual's self-confidence and faith that he has potential of performing the task. Higher the level of self-efficiency, greater will be the efforts put in by the individual when they face challenging tasks. While, lower the level of self-efficiency, less will be the efforts put in by the individual or he might even quit while meeting challenges.

    b. **Goal commitment-** Goal setting theory assumes that the individual is committed to the goal and will not leave the goal. The goal commitment is dependent on the following factors:

        i.   Goals are made open, known and broadcasted.

        ii.   Goals should bc sct-sclf by individual rather than designated.

        iii.   Individual's set goals should be consistent with the organizational goals and vision.

Advantages of Goal Setting Theory

- Goal setting theory is a technique used to raise incentives for employees to complete work quickly and effectively.

- Goal setting leads to better performance by increasing motivation and efforts, but also through increasing and improving the feedback quality.

Limitations of Goal Setting Theory

- At times, the organizational goals are in conflict with the managerial goals. Goal conflict has a detrimental effect on the performance if it motivates incompatible action drift.

- Very difficult and complex goals stimulate riskier behaviour.

- If the employee lacks skills and competencies to perform actions essential for goal, then the goal-setting can fail and lead to undermining of performance.

- There is no evidence to prove that goal-setting improves job satisfaction.

Reinforcement Theory of Motivation

Reinforcement theory of motivation was proposed by BF Skinner and his associates. It states that individual's behaviour is a function of its consequences. It is based on "law of effect", i.e, individual's behaviour with positive consequences tends to be repeated, but individual's behaviour with negative consequences tends not to be repeated.

Reinforcement theory of motivation overlooks the internal state of individual, i.e., the inner feelings and drives of individuals are ignored by Skinner. This theory focuses totally on what happens to an individual when he takes some action. Thus, according to Skinner, the external environment of the organization must be designed effectively and positively so as to motivate the employee. This theory is a strong tool for analyzing controlling mechanism for individual's behaviour. However, it does not focus on the causes of individual's behaviour.

The managers use the following methods for controlling the behaviour of the employees:

Positive Reinforcement- This implies giving a positive response when an individual shows positive and required behaviour. For example - Immediately praising an employee for coming early for job. This will increase probability of outstanding behaviour occurring again. Reward is a positive reinforce, but not necessarily. If and only if the employees' behaviour improves, reward can said to be a positive reinforcer. Positive reinforcement stimulates occurrence of a behaviour. It must be noted that more spontaneous is the giving of reward, the greater reinforcement value it has.

Negative Reinforcement- This implies rewarding an employee by removing negative / undesirable consequences. Both positive and negative reinforcement can be used for increasing desirable / required behaviour.

Punishment- It implies removing positive consequences so as to lower the probability of repeating undesirable behaviour in future. In other words, punishment means applying undesirable consequence for showing undesirable behaviour. For instance - Suspending an employee for breaking the organizational rules. Punishment can be equalized by positive reinforcement from alternative source.

Extinction- It implies absence of reinforcements. In other words, extinction implies lowering the probability of undesired behaviour by removing reward for that kind of behaviour. For instance - if an employee no longer receives praise and admiration for his good work, he may feel that his behaviour is generating no fruitful consequence. Extinction may unintentionally lower desirable behaviour.

Implications of Reinforcement Theory

Reinforcement theory explains in detail how an individual learns behaviour. Managers who are making attempt to motivate the employees must ensure that they do not reward all employees simultaneously. They must tell the employees what they are not doing correct. They must tell the employees how they can achieve positive reinforcement.

McClelland's Theory of Needs

David McClelland and his associates proposed McClelland's theory of Needs / Achievement Motivation Theory. This theory states that human behaviour is affected by three needs - Need for Power, Achievement and Affiliation. Need for **achievement** is the urge to excel, to accomplish in relation to a set of standards, to struggle to achieve success. Need for **power** is the desire to influence other individual's behaviour as per your wish. In other words, it is the desire to have control over others and to be influential. Need for **affiliation** is a need for open and sociable interpersonal relationships. In other words, it is a desire for relationship based on co-operation and mutual understanding.

The individuals with high achievement needs are highly motivated by competing and challenging work. They look for promotional opportunities in job. They have a strong urge for feedback on their achievement. Such individuals try to get satisfaction in performing things better. High achievement is directly related to high performance. Individuals who are better and above average performers are highly motivated. They assume responsibility for solving the problems at work. McClelland called such individuals as gamblers as they set challenging targets

for themselves and they take deliberate risk to achieve those set targets. Such individuals look for innovative ways of performing job. They perceive achievement of goals as a reward, and value it more than a financial reward.

The individuals who are motivated by power have a strong urge to be influential and controlling. They want that their views and ideas should dominate and thus, they want to lead. Such individuals are motivated by the need for reputation and self-esteem. Individuals with greater power and authority will perform better than those possessing less power. Generally, managers with high need for power turn out to be more efficient and successful managers. They are more determined and loyal to the organization they work for. Need for power should not always be taken negatively. It can be viewed as the need to have a positive effect on the organization and to support the organization in achieving it's goals.

The individuals who are motivated by affiliation have an urge for a friendly and supportive environment. Such individuals are effective performers in a team. These people want to be liked by others. The manager's ability to make decisions is hampered if they have a high affiliation need as they prefer to be accepted and liked by others, and this weakens their objectivity. Individuals having high affiliation needs prefer working in an environment providing greater personal interaction. Such people have a need to be on the good books of all. They generally cannot be good leaders.

Reinforcement Theory of Motivation

Reinforcement theory of motivation was proposed by BF Skinner and his associates. It states that individual's behaviour is a function of its consequences. It is based on "law of effect", i.e, individual's behaviour with positive consequences tends to be repeated, but individual's behaviour with negative consequences tends not to be repeated.

Reinforcement theory of motivation overlooks the internal state of individual, i.e., the inner feelings and drives of individuals are ignored by Skinner. This theory focuses totally on what happens to an individual when he takes some action. Thus, according to Skinner, the external environment of the organization must be designed effectively and positively so as to motivate the employee. This theory is a strong tool for analyzing controlling mechanism for individual's behaviour. However, it does not focus on the causes of individual's behaviour.

The managers use the following methods for controlling the behaviour of the employees:

✓ **Positive Reinforcement-** This implies giving a positive response when an individual shows positive and required behaviour. For example - Immediately praising an employee for coming early for job. This will increase probability of outstanding behaviour occurring again. Reward is a positive reinforce, but not necessarily. If and only if the employees' behaviour improves, reward can said to be a positive reinforcer. Positive reinforcement stimulates occurrence of a behaviour. It must be noted that more spontaneous is the giving of reward, the greater reinforcement value it has.

✓ **Negative Reinforcement-** This implies rewarding an employee by removing negative / undesirable consequences. Both positive and negative reinforcement can be used for increasing desirable / required behaviour.

✓ **Punishment-** It implies removing positive consequences so as to lower the probability of repeating undesirable behaviour in future. In other words, punishment means applying undesirable consequence for showing undesirable behaviour. For instance - Suspending an employee for breaking the organizational rules. Punishment can be equalized by positive reinforcement from alternative source.

✓ **Extinction-** It implies absence of reinforcements. In other words, extinction implies lowering the probability of undesired behaviour by removing reward for that kind of behaviour. For instance - if an employee no longer receives praise and admiration for his good work, he may feel that his behaviour is generating no fruitful consequence. Extinction may unintentionally lower desirable behaviour.

Implications of Reinforcement Theory

Reinforcement theory explains in detail how an individual learns behaviour. Managers who are making attempt to motivate the employees must ensure that they do not reward all employees simultaneously. They must tell the employees what they are not doing correct. They must tell the employees how they can achieve positive reinforcement.

Equity Theory of Motivation

The core of the equity theory is the principle of balance or equity. As per this motivation theory, an individual's motivation level is correlated to his perception of equity, fairness and justice practiced by the management. Higher is individual's perception of fairness, greater is the motivation level and vice versa. While evaluating fairness, employee compares the job input (in terms of contribution) to outcome (in terms of compensation) and also compares the same with that of another peer of equal cadre/category. D/I ratio (output-input ratio) is used to make such a comparison.

EQUITY THEORY

Ratio Comparison	Perception
O/I a < O/I b	Under-rewarded (Equity Tension)
O/I a = O/I b	Equity
O/I a > O/I b	Over-rewarded (Equity

Tension)

Negative Tension state: Equity is perceived when this ratio is equal. While if this ratio is unequal, it leads to "equity tension". J.Stacy Adams called this a negative tension state which motivates him to do something right to relieve this tension. A comparison has been made between 2 workers A and B to understand this point.

Referents: The four comparisons an employee can make have been termed as "referents" according to Goodman. The referent chosen is a significant variable in equity theory. These referents are as follows:

- Self-inside: An employee's experience in a different position inside his present organization.

- Self-outside: An employee's experience in a situation outside the present organization.

- Other-inside: Another employee or group of employees inside the employee's present organization.

- Other-outside: Another employee or employees outside the employee's present organization.

An employee might compare himself with his peer within the present job in the current organization or with his friend/peer working in some other organization or with the past jobs held by him with others. An employee's choice of the referent will be influenced by the appeal of the referent and the employee's knowledge about the referent.

Moderating Variables: The gender, salary, education and the experience level are moderating variables. Individuals with greater and higher education are more informed. Thus, they are likely to compare themselves with the outsiders. Males and females prefer same sex comparison. It has been observed that females are paid typically less than males in comparable jobs and have less salary expectations than male for the same work. Thus, a women employee that uses another women employee as a referent tends to lead to a lower comparative standard. Employees with greater experience know their organization very well and compare themselves with their own colleagues, while employees with less experience rely on their personal experiences and knowledge for making comparisons.

Choices: The employees who perceive inequity and are under negative tension can make the following choices:

✓ Change in input (e.g. Don't overexert)

✓ Change their outcome (Produce quantity output and increasing earning by sacrificing quality when piece rate incentive system exist)

✓ Choose a different referent

✓ Quit the job

✓ Change self perception (For instance - I know that I've performed better and harder than everyone else.)

✓ Change perception of others (For instance - Jack's job is not as desirable as I earlier thought it was.)

Assumptions of the Equity Theory

- The theory demonstrates that the individuals are concerned both with their own rewards and also with what others get in their comparison.

- Employees expect a fair and equitable return for their contribution to their jobs.

- Employees decide what their equitable return should be after comparing their inputs and outcomes with those of their colleagues.

- Employees who perceive themselves as being in an inequitable scenario will attempt to reduce the inequity either by distorting inputs and/or outcomes psychologically, by directly altering inputs and/or outputs, or by quitting the organization.

Expectancy Theory of Motivation

The expectancy theory was proposed by **Victor Vroom** of Yale School of Management in 1964. Vroom stresses and focuses on outcomes, and not on needs unlike Maslow and Herzberg. The theory states that the intensity of a tendency to perform in a particular manner is dependent on the intensity of an expectation that the performance will be followed by a definite outcome and on the appeal of the outcome to the individual.

The **Expectancy theory** states that employee's motivation is an outcome of how much an individual wants a reward (Valence), the assessment that the likelihood that the effort will lead to expected performance (Expectancy) and the belief that the performance will lead to reward (Instrumentality). In short, **Valence** is the significance associated by an individual about the expected outcome. It is an expected and not the actual satisfaction that an employee expects to receive after achieving the goals. **Expectancy** is the faith that better efforts will result in better performance. Expectancy is influenced by factors such as possession of appropriate skills for performing the job, availability of right resources, availability of crucial information and getting the required support for completing the job.

Instrumentality is the faith that if you perform well, then a valid outcome will be there. Instrumentality is affected by factors such as believe in the people who decide who receives what outcome, the simplicity of the process deciding who gets what outcome, and clarity of relationship between performance and outcomes. Thus, the expectancy theory concentrates on the following three relationships:

- Effort-performance relationship: What is the likelihood that the individual's effort be recognized in his performance appraisal?

- Performance-reward relationship: It talks about the extent to which the employee believes that getting a good performance appraisal leads to organizational rewards.

- Rewards-personal goals relationship: It is all about the attractiveness or appeal of the potential reward to the individual.

Vroom was of view that employees consciously decide whether to perform or not at the job. This decision solely depended on the employee's motivation level which in turn depends on three factors of expectancy, valence and instrumentality.

Advantages of the Expectancy Theory

- It is based on self-interest individual who want to achieve maximum satisfaction and who wants to minimize dissatisfaction.

- This theory stresses upon the expectations and perception; what is real and actual is immaterial.

- It emphasizes on rewards or pay-offs. It focuses on psychological extravagance where final objective of individual is to attain maximum pleasure and least pain.

Limitations of the Expectancy Theory

- The expectancy theory seems to be idealistic because quite a few individuals perceive high degree correlation between performance and rewards.

- The application of this theory is limited as reward is not directly correlated with performance in many organizations. It is related to other parameters also such as position, effort, responsibility, education, etc.

Implications of the Expectancy Theory

The managers can correlate the preferred outcomes to the aimed performance levels.

The managers must ensure that the employees can achieve the aimed performance levels.

The deserving employees must be rewarded for their exceptional performance.

The reward system must be fair and just in an organization.

Organizations must design interesting, dynamic and

challenging jobs.

The employee's motivation level should be continually assessed through various techniques such as questionnaire, personal interviews, etc.